OH I

Best wishes
Dad S
x x

DOUGLAS M. SMITH

ISBN: 9798609279262

An Inherit The Earth Publication 2020 ©
In conjunction with Amazon.

Edited by CT Meek.

Foreword.

It has been a dream of Dougie's for some time to have his book published. He has been a regular contributor to the collaborative writing project For The Many Not The Few, which is now up to Volume 13 (at the time of writing). Dougie hails from Carronshore, once a thriving mining village, in the Falkirk area of Scotland. The village sits North of the River Carron. It has always been a pleasure to work with Dougie and I hope he goes on to write many more pieces.

CT Meek.
February 2020.

Contents.

Wee Tam.

Oh what a sleep that was,
I better get oot ma bed,
I just heard my mum's voice shouting,
move it sleepy head
Up I get, the hoose is cauld,
freezin' on my toes,
I put my dressing gown on quick
and grab hold of my clothes

I rush downstairs as fast as I can; this winter is so
dire,
I throw my clothes doon and there we are, in front
of my wee fire,
I get up and put the telly on, Saturday morning fun
It's champion the wonder horse, and Uncle Sandy
with his gun

My mum shouts here's yer breakfast, come and get
it right away - Aww ya beauty,
A roll on square, wi broon sauce on it tae
I'm ready now, oot tae play, I'm going for wee Tam
and see what we can find to do, excited noo I am,
So roond I walked, half a mile, a wee hole in my
shoe
and I shoulda stuck the sole on better, wi ma
Faither's glue

I chap Tam's door and what a fricht, another lad was there
 I said to him, Is Tam comin' oot, he just gave me a stare
Wha are you pal, what's yer game, this is what he said, The Tam that lived here long ago, he's been 43 years dead It was like a bombshell, flippin' heck it can't be true
Come in said the wee laddie, the door I ventured through

Your house, it's so warm, and it smells so nice like flowers in yer hall
He pointed and said, air fresheners are plugged into the wall
I asked him what his name was; he said his name was Sam
and he said that he had heard the story, all about wee Tam
He drowned one winter's day ye see in 1975
And his wee pal tried to save him; I think he's still alive
We went into his bedroom, and holy moly mother
He had a bedroom like the shows, like I haven't seen another

A colour telly, and a bed sae braw, and arcade games as well
on his ain big massive screen, I'm thinking bloody hell

And that thing in his hand noo, what the heck is that,

Black and shiny, making noises, and very small and flat

What's that I asked, is it a game, I've no seen one like this

He looked at me, it's ma mobile phone pal, you taking the piss?

He said watch this I'll show you and he said then hello mam.

Goan bring up my breakfast, a roll on crispy ham

Then five minutes later his maw appears with a roll and can of Irn Bru

If I'd asked my mam to do that, she'd have telt me what to do

This was all so weird ye ken, you should have seen his clothes

Very posh... an fitbaw bits, a' lined up in rows,

yellow ones and blue ones, that come up roond yer ankle

I couldn't even put them on without getting in a fankle

I said to him, ye comin oot? He said what dae ye mean

I said well comin out tae play? Ye Dinna seem too keen

We can make a Tarzan swing ye Ken, or play at Chicky Mellie

or go roond the roond aboot a hundred times

till ye wobble like a jelly

or let's play at Grand National, or what about chap door run
Naw said Sam, I'm playing my x box, it's far far better fun
I looked at him with disappointment; in a fancy chair he sat
He looked an awful lazy boy, and just a wee bit fat
Well I said, I'm goin' home, I need to see my mam
I want tae tell her a' that's happened and a' aboot wee Tam

I ran home quick and slammed the door and I tried to tell my mam
About my morning so so strange, but she was very calm
She said it's ok pal, settle down, ye just had a wee blast
Of what the future holds for you, now get back tae the past
Just then a noise so loud and shrill, blasted in my ears
I opened my eyes and sat upright and wiped away the tears
and ,am shouted come on you, yer lazy to the core
Yer breakfast's oot and the telly's on and wee Tam's at the door
I rushed downstairs to see my pal, he said ye comin out
We can go down tae the pond the day and have a play about

Well, my heart sank, and I said no way, let's makes a Tarzan swing
or play at fitba or chap door run, any bloody thing
My pal was here, and he wouldn't drown, things aren't as they seem
The day the present met the past, in my horrific dream.

(*Author's Note* - This poem came to life as I began writing it, and when I got to the end I was quite emotional. This is the poem that inspired the book.)

Facebook.

Oh well, time to get up and see what's going on
Clicking onto Facebook at the crack of bloody dawn
There we are, sorted, and my profiles loaded up,
Just pouring my coffee noo, in my favourite cup
Now... what's the goss, let me see,
Noo I've started scrolling

Willie he's been at the gym and Derek's at the
bowling Poor wee Jimmy lost his mum I better send
a heart
And there's wee Erin passed her test,
Awww she's awfy smart

Jeanie seems so angry, the quotes she's putting up
And there's wee Morag went awa and got hersel a
pup Dan's in a relationship, I wonder who it's with?
Awww it's someone fi the boag there,
Her name is Margaret Smith
Noo I should really know her
As I look at mutual friends
I hope they're really happy, suppose it just depends

Awww and here's Theresa may now,
I better have a glance
Omg she's with a tribe and doin' a funny dance
Eddies drunk as usual, he's out with Frank and
Joacky Singin' Folsom Prison Blues on the karaoke

Oh, and here I've got a friend request,
Awww shit, just my luck
From Abdul Assie from Oman
Well he can get TAE Falkirk

Jim and Mary aww how nice, out with their wee dugs, posting selfies at the park, showing off their mugs
Wee Annie got engaged there, and Rab is feeling sad
And there's big Andy on his birthday posin' with his dad

Bloody hell, Gordon Haining,
He's gone and pooped his pants

Awww but haud on just a minute,
He's at the works big dance
I know what's happened there then,
He's been up there for a boogie
And one of the lads has gone and fraped him,
Probably his mate Dougie

Awww well, I'm all caught up, better move my ass
Got my keys? Got my piece? My wallet and my pass
Oh, before I leave the house, I'll put up a wee post
I'll tell them a' I had my coffee and marmite oan ma toast.
Have a Guid day everyone, hi ho hi ho hi ho
Signing off from Facebook noo, off to work I go

(*Author's Note -* This poem is dedicated to my oldest Facebook friend and a family that lived opposite us as we grew up in the mining village of Carronshore. Sandra Collumbine with her husband Ernie. The picture taken at the wee flat they used to take us on our holidays when we were wee. Respect.)

Photos On Your Wall.

How can a picture say so much
Just hanging on your wall
A thought that just occurred to me
Whilst walking through the hall

So down I sit and look around
At Family photographs
And think about my family, our lives
The love the laughs

A generation gone now,
My darling mum and dad
Standing on their wedding day
It makes me feel quite sad
I touch the picture lovingly
A tear runs down my cheek
I pass this picture every day
A hundred times a week

Then there are my grandparents
Gone a long long while
Looking at me, haunting eyes
In black and white they smile

An aunt I had, I loved so much
Like a second Mam
My nephews and my niece as well
I'm proud of them, I am

And then I think about it all
And how fragile life can be
All these pictures tell a tale
Each one talks to me

And years from now, on someone's wall
I'll be hanging too
With a million stories, if I were there
That I could tell to you

I get up from my chair now,
And carry on my day
The pictures hang there silently,
A million things to say

Live each day like it's your last
And keep your kinfolk near
Tell them that you love them
Tell them when they're here

Because some day in the future
You'll be on someone's wall
And you can't tell them anything;
Anything at all

Life is precious, life is fragile
Life is short and sweet
Smile as you walk past a stranger
Walking down your street

Say please and thank you
Hold a door, doesn't have to be a fuss
Give your seat to some old lady
Sitting on the bus

Family is everything, the best thing by a mile
So make sure when you pass your pictures
Look at them ......
And smile

(*Author's Note -* The Poem says it all, this is a photo of my Father, Alex Smith with his skiffle band, The Tom Cats, far right on the washboard.)

The Greatest Gift Of All.

Remember all those feelings,
You had when you were wee
The presents all wrapped up so nice,
Underneath the tree
And remember putting out the milk
And cakes on Christmas Eve
A magical time, an innocent time,
A time when you believe
Trying to sleep, so restless,
Listening for the sleigh
Jingling and jangling
As it makes its merry way
Then up you get so early,
And run downstairs so fast
After waiting on your mummy,
But now she's up at last
And then you see your presents
You can't believe your eyes
Parcels beautifully wrapped
And every shape and size
An action man, a cowboy hat,
And sweets and other stuff
Spoiled rotten, Santa doesn't know
Just when you've had enough
And when you've opened all your gifts
And feeling so so thrilled
All your list has been delivered
All your dreams fulfilled

But here's the thing I wanted to say
The thing you didn't know

The thing that made your Christmas,
The thing that made it so
The greatest gift you ever had,
T'was there year after year
And you didn't know, and never will,
Until the gifts not here
It was there on Christmas Eve you know,
Before old Santa came
And it was also there on Christmas night,
And Boxing Day the same
And one day when you're older,
You'll look back and see
That Christmas time is when the gift,
Takes care of you and me
You see, the gifts your mummy,
The greatest gift of all
Better than an action man

And better than a doll
My mummy isn't here now,
And every Christmas day
I close my eyes and remember back,
And quietly I say
Thank you mum for being there,
I miss you at this time
But I'm so glad I had you,
Glad that you were mine
Your heart was huge, a funny thing,
Cause you were very small
I want to tell you mum,
You were the greatest gift of all.

(**Author's Note -** My Mother, Elizabeth Jean Duncan
Smith. The Poem says it all. Missed every day.)

The Last Man Standing.

I used to pass a man each day
As I walked down my street
And I always thought of him
As one of Carronshore's elite

Not once did this man pass me by
Without that smile so fine
As he walked down on his side
And I walked up on mine

A gentleman, who in my book,
Will always stand so tall
And one that I will think of,
When I think of Quarrolhall

He'd meet up with his pals each day,
And with their dogs they'd walk
And bring to life the days gone by,
As they would laugh and talk

They'd put the world to rights you see,
And talk of its disgrace
And if these men were put in charge
It'd be a better place

This group of gents grew smaller,
As the years and years went by

For old dogs and their masters,
Eventually die.

And now the last man standing,
The one from Quarrolhall,
Has left us and went up to heaven,
United with them all.

He left behind two daughters,
That I've known a long long while
And you know, that when I pass them
I see their daddy's smile

That's the gift he gave them,
And what a gift indeed
This man was a gent you see -
A special kind of breed.

One of a kind, a dad and husband,
Kind and understanding,
And Mr Mclay, until this day
You were... the last man standing

And you left a mark with this wee boy
That passed you in the street
And you inspired him to give a smile
To everyone he'd meet.

For Linda and Wilma.

(*Author's Note* - This gentleman used to pass our house every day, and he was... a Gentleman, I read on social media that he had passed away through his daughters post, and I realised that he had touched my heart, within 10 minutes I had written. The Last Man Standing and it's a tribute to the gift of smiling and a tribute to a Carronshore legend.)

The Monarch Of The Glen.

He stands there so majestically,
As proud as he could be
Scotland's pride and glory,
Of that we all agree

You'll see him at the roadside,
You'll see him on the Ben
A sight that takes your breath away,
The Monarch of the Glen

The bonnie purple heather
And the raging bubbling streams
The bracken and the waterfalls,
Beyond your wildest dreams

The mountains in the winter,
Covered white with snow
Beauty at its very best,
From Oban to Glencoe

All these views are beautiful,
And on postcards awww sae sweet
But it takes the Monarch of the Glen
To make the scene complete

Master of the highlands,
He has nae need tae brag

He just stands there, so big and strong,
The beast they call the stag

And if you're lucky enough to see him,
Who knows where or when
Get oot yer car and take a bow,
To the Monarch of the Glen.

The Fox.

The sly old Fox, he slinks away,
He night times now turned into day

Another hour the Dawn will break
And that's when all the humans wake

A funny breed and different kinds
They try to boggle wi' oor minds

Some will give us scraps o' food
Chicken, meat, awww they're awfy good

If only they were all the same
This life would be a better game

But some are evil, oot tae kill
They try to shoot us at their will

For what; for trying to live?
Not a thought do these folk give

And these pompous cretins use their forces
Chasing us while oan their horses

Wi' packs o' dogs, fit and smart
That want to tear oor limbs apart

They're what we cry God's disgrace
The bastards of the human race

Anyway, I better go, it's getting light
It's been another tough auld night

The way we live, from day to day
It's hard and there's no other way

The war o' life imposed by men
At least we're safe, back in oor den

Warm and snug and oot o' sight
Till we go back out tomorrow night

Slinking slyly from the den
To seek survival once again.

The Sweeper.

Time to come home son it's getting dark
The wee boy playing fitba at Burnside Park

Granny Wilson's calling Ernie,
He's been kicking that ba' all day

The laddie loved his football, and by Jove he could
play

Brilliant in midfield,
Could play on the wing, brilliant as a keeper,

Could score goals for fun, great in defence,
And was Britain's first known sweeper

This Burnside laddie turned into
The most beautiful loving man
And everyone who knew him,
Turned out to be a fan

He lived the most amazing life,
Family to the core
And it hurts that we won't get to see
That big smile any more

He was the skipper of the family, loved by
everyone,
The grandkids loved him

Through and through
And they had so much fun
He taught them to sing the Glesga Cat song
And the one about the Collumbine as they drove
along

Cruising down the motorway at forty miles an hour
We are the family Collumbine; we are a hard up
shower
We ain't got no money no not us
We'll soon have to take the bloody bus

Yes, our Ernie was talented and gifted like no other
A beautiful husband a dad,
An uncle a neighbour and a brother

But a voice was calling once again,
Just like at the park
Granny Wilson calling him,
Come on it's getting dark

And Ernie's now gone home you know,
His life is now complete
He's ran home like he used to do,
The ba' still at his feet

The Carronshore legend, friend of yours and mine
We'll never forget you, you were the best
Ernie Collumbine.

Buckie's Just The Best.

As I roam the Moray Sand
The brawest in the land Frae
Cullen Bay and Buckie
Findochty ah sae grand
As I think of days gan by,
It brings a teardrop tae my eye

Portknockie Harbour sits there,
With bonnie boats sae braw
I've never known such beauty,
It would take yer breath awa

Lossie, Elgin Fochabers,
And Buckie aye sae fine
Ye ken it wid steal yer heart awa,
It's gan and stolen mine

The Doric language still alive,
So beautiful to hear
Fit like an how you doing
A drammie or a beer

Are ye goin doon tae the shoppie,
Tae get a buttery roll sae braw
Or a softie wi' some jam on it
For that's the best of aw

The quines and loons are magic
And I love their Doric race
And every time I hear it spoke
A smile lights up my face

The boaties bobbing up and down
In the early morning haar
Waiting for their hardened crew
Tae take them oot sae far

Chasing a' the herring
And the shrimps and crabbies too
The fishermen sae weatherbeat
Are tough men through and through

My childhood memories warm my heart,
As I think of bygone days
My auntie Pat and Frances,
And all their loving ways

A bed here ony time ye Ken,
And bring the bairnies too
There's aye a place here ye can bide
There's aye a bed for you

The Moray Firth sae beautiful
But Buckie's just the best
My family there aye make sure
There's nae unwanted guest

So if ye want tae come up for a break
And see this bonnie land
Morayshire will welcome you
A place that's oh so grand.

Auschwitz.

Doom, doom, doom,
This is now our lives
Separated at the gate
They took away our wives

We now all wear our uniforms,
Pyjamas so so rough
Any day could be our last,
We all have had enough

My friend Olaf, I miss him so,
We shared our innermost
Until that bastard SS man,
Put him against a post

Olaf looked into my eyes,
I couldn't do a thing
I knew for him it was the end
The Guard had heard him sing

Bang, Olaf was now saved from this
At peace and no more pain
Just another Jewish man,
Innocent yet slain

I headed back to the block I share
With 400 poor souls
Hungarian, Jewish, Belgian too

And then my own, the Poles
The smell would make you faint you know
And the muffled sound of tears
Grown men crying, spirits broken
All they have now is their fears

Down I lie and think of Olaf,
And then I understood
He had had enough of this abhorrence
And he escaped, the way he could

Sidling to that gestapo man,
He cleared his aching throat, and then
Sang proudly Hava Nagila,
Oh my brave and trusted friend

Olaf, I didn't even know his surname,
And many times I've cried
But when he sang his Jewish song
I knew his spirit hadn't died

Those murdering evil Nazi soldiers
And their murderous evil plan
Is the biggest show of Man's inhumanity to man.

Oor Wullie.

Well his name is Wullie McCallum,
Frae Auchenshuggle Town
He was famous when he was a lad,
Aye ways playin' the clown

He was aye getting' intae bother,
Aye ways hain a laugh
And Sunday nights his ma just couldnae
Get him in the bath

And it's crivvens jeepers help ma boab,
And by Jove, michty me
Wullie's a' grown up noo,
Of that we'll have to see
Wi his catapult and tackety bits,
An Jeemy his wee moose
And yid aye see him sittin' on his bucket,
Just outside his hoose

Well and day no sae long ago,
Wi Primrose for a date
It's no like in the teenage years
When he used to master fitba
He took her tae the Regal,
Then the Clachan for a beer
And when she agreed to be his burd,
He smiled fae ear to ear

Well Friday night out wi the lads,
For a pint or two or three
Auld Daphne Broon was in the corner,
What a lass was she

Well Fat Boab he was steaming,
And he thought he'd ask her oot
But Soapy, Eck an Wullie, shouted Naw,
She's just a boot

Well the nicht drave on and they were pissed
Night had turned into day
And the five o' them woke up together
At the bottom o' Stoorie Brae

Noo PC Murdoch saw them there,
A' lying in the grass
He thocht it was another hill,
But it was just big Daphne's arse

Well when wee Primrose heard o' this,
She chucked Oor Wullie then
Wullie shouted please wee Primrose,
I've done nothing hen

We just went for a walk ye see,
Walkin' Daphne hame
Then Soapy got the whisky out,
So it's really him tae blame

And as we sat there drinking,
We must have fell asleep
Pished out of our minds hen
And lying in a heap

The next thing Murdoch woke us up,
Just oor bloody luck
He stuck his boot up Soapy's arse
And shouted get tae fuck

So Primrose she forgave him,
She said it was ok
She also said there's something, Wullie,
That I have tae say

When you were oot wi the lads last night,
I fulfilled a fantasy
I had the Boaby in my hoose,
'Cause Murdoch.....was ....with me......

Ghost Train (Short Story).

All was quiet at Misty View, the windows boasted the most beautiful patterns you could ever see, sparkling and dancing in the morning sun, it was a cold October morning and Douglas turned over in his bed, thinking of getting up and the dash down the stairs to the coal fire. He could hear his mum Liz pottering about in the scullery.

Douglas was a dreamer, ever since his Father left to go and fight in the war, Douglas imagined him shooting the evil men from the Gestapo, he would tell his friends his dad was a war hero and took out full units of Nazis single- headedly.

His mum had told him years before that his amazing war hero dad was missing in action presumed dead. Douglas never accepted this and believed deep in his faithful heart that his dad would one day walk the short distance from the train station in Forfar, up the steep hill to Misty View.

It was Halloween 1949 and today Douglas was going to visit his Aunt Polly in Dundee. She didn't really get about much so Douglas visited every fortnight, going on the train and taking her a bag of her favourite soor plooms, he always waited till he was leaving before he presented Aunt Polly with the sweets, as he couldn't bare the noise they made, rattling of her false teeth.

Douglas got up, snatched his clothes from the chair and ran down the stairs to the roaring fire.

Morning son, Liz called from ben the house; do you want porridge this morning?

Aye please Mum, porridge was his favourite, especially on a freezing cold Autumn morning.

The radio was playing Al Jolson and Sonny Boy; Douglas loves his music and would sit glued to the big radio set for hours.

Half an hour later he was walking down the brae, he had a wee packed lunch which consisted of a slice of hard porridge (his piece) and an apple and a boiled egg.

Mum was waving at the door, she always looked sad and tired, her hair was up with a towel and she had her pinny on and a cigarette dangling from her lips. Be careful son. Douglas waved back, he just adored his mum and wished he could make her smile the way she used to when dad put his big strong arms round her and swung her round. The thought made Douglas smile.

Douglas walked along singing run rabbit run, a popular song in school.

The sun had disappeared very quickly behind a very heavy mist. Visibility was poor as he walked slowly into the desolate wee station.

He sat in the waiting room and it was really warm, Douglas put his head on the padded seats, he was still a bit tired as he had sat up half the night listening to the radio.

Suddenly a very loud whistle echoed through the station and Douglas got a terrible fright.

He rushed out onto the platform and saw the ticket man with his flag, waving him into the open door. He looked very, very serious and didn't say a word. The train was long and black, but strangely silent.

Douglas walked up the carriage and was both confused and intrigued; the train was full of soldiers, with uniforms just like his dads.

He sat in a booth beside three soldiers playing cards, none of them looked at him, the one sitting next to him took off his hat and Douglas saw a large wound and a small trickle of blood ran down his cheek.

From further up the carriage there were men singing songs loudly, pack up your troubles in your old kit bag and smile, smile, smile......

The train rumbled on not stopping at any of the stations, Douglas was scared, this wasn't right; the men kept playing cards and not one of them even looked at him.

They were smoking cigarettes and one of them had a bottle of rum and they all took a swig.

The train got faster and faster, the horn blew, very loud, the men were singing louder and louder, it's a long way to Tipperary it's a long way to go....

Douglas got up to use the toilet, he was very afraid, the train was now going so fast he could hardly walk up the aisle, the noise was deafening, the train was smoky and smelt of sweat and a funny smell that he decided was blood.

He fell down and as he stood up he noticed the cubicle next to him had four men singing songs, one of the men had only one arm, and the far away one had no face, just eyes, big blue eyes with tears flowing from them dripping onto his army jacket.

The other two both had head wounds as well, Douglas looked around, the train was full of these soldiers, all injured, all missing limbs and faces covered in blood, the train was now hammering along, the singing was deafening. There'll be blue birds over, the white cliffs of
Dover...

Douglas got to the toilet door and almost collapsed as a young blonde haired Sergeant walked straight through a solid door. He crouched down in front of Douglas and smiled, he said Dinny worry wee man, it's goin tae be fine son, and he winked.

The train hammered on through a tunnel, it was pitch dark but the soldiers were illuminated and were singing and cheering, the horn blew really loud and Douglas put his hands over his ears, the tears ran down his face and he screamed as loudly as he could....heeeeeelllllppppp me.....

Just then everything fell silent, Douglas opened his eyes, he was back in the waiting room in the train station, the whistle blew and the train pulled away, Douglas wouldn't be seeing Aunt Polly today....

He had had the most awful Halloween nightmare, and he wanted his mum, as he walked away from the station, someone shouted....Douglas. Is that you?

From the mist came a figure, he walked with crutches and
his left leg was missing from the knee down..,,

Douglas looked at him closely, he thought he was dreaming again, dad? Is it you? Is it really you?

Aye it's me son, I've had amnesia and I've been ill, but I'm home. Douglas dropped his bag and rushed towards his hero, tears blinding him.

They walked up the brae and Liz was at the back step clapping Lassie the black lab, she looked, she screamed with delight, she rushed down the steps and threw her arms round her husband.

Everything was going to be ok.

Then; Liz shook Douglas, come on son, get up, you're going to Dundee today to see Polly.....

It was a Halloween dream he'd never forget.

Silver Thread.

The man was singing, silver threads
Like any other song
It was in a care home in Dunoon
He wouldn't be there long
But as he sang, his eyes locked
With a lovely lady there
Sitting with a bib on,
Aith her straggly short white hair
Her face was sinking, veins showed through
It was really such a sin
And she mouthed the words, thank you son
With slavers down her chin

And the man looked right into her soul
And the words of the song came true
And for a moment, the lady changed
And was young and fresh and new

You see this lady's been here a while
And had a long long life
She's been a child, she's been a sister
A mother and a wife

Her eyes now sparkled,
And her hair was blonde
And fell down on her shoulder
She never thought this could be her
When she had gotten older

Her lips were red and full and nice
Her teeth they shone so white
And her shape was lovely, buxom,
A Bonnie, Bonnie sight
A tear fell down the singer's cheek,
As the last verse took its place
This lady was on her last verse too
He seen it in her face

Darling you are growing old,
There's a silver thread among the gold

But my darling you will be,
Always young and dear to me

And as the man was leaving,
He hugged this lady tight,
And kissed her on the cheek and told her,
She had made his night

The tears ran down her withered cheeks
And then they said goodbye
And he left her sitting in her chair
Knowing she'd soon die

Don't forget our old folks
They once were just like you
And one day if you're lucky
You'll get older like them too
Give them a hug, a kiss, a smile
Sing for them a song
Hold their hand, squeeze it gently
They won't be with us long.

(**Author's Note -** This poem was written at the side of Loch Eck in Argyll, on my way home from playing at an old folks home, a beautiful old lady aged 93 touched my heart that day.)

The World's Disgrace.

Rat-a-tat-tat, rat-a-tat-tat
The sound of evil that was that
The Nazi soldiers leather boots
That matched their Hugo Boss army suits
On that bygone dreadful day
They've come to take the Jews away

From the ghettos if they survive
If they've been allowed to stay alive
Old men young men babies too
Young girls old girls any Jew

They round us up, men so insane
And load us all into the train
Freezing cold, and clothes so damp
Bound for the concentration camp

Where all my kinfolk on this date
Will go with me to meet our fate

Innocent people, that's what we are
Trundling along in every car

And then the train stops, whistles blow
Achtung they shout... It's time to go

We knew it would be our last hour
As we got ready for our shower

Remember us, this Jewish race
And the Nazi soldiers... The worlds disgrace.

What Will My Next Meal Be?

What will my next meal be?
What excitement lies in store?
I look into my larder
Ohhhh, there's half an apple, and more
And there is some beer left in that tin
And jackpot! A plastic carton, heavy, win win
That means food,
Going to be a good day
It might be very tasty, maybe not
I'm going to eat it anyway

I'll sit down for a bit and watch the folk
And how they live makes me boak
Laces in their shoes, and clothes that smell like new
I remember when I was a child, mine were like that
too

A guy he sees me, he looks happy, witty
I see the look, the look of pity
He gestures, wait here, I'll be back in two
And off he runs, the way they do

Wonder what he'll bring me today
Does he talk like me? What will I say?

Eggs and bread, nice, I look at the man
Jink, and move on fast as I can

I must be such a dreadful sight
As I rake the buckets, and fight my fight
Don't take your food and lives for granted
I was once like you
A few bits of bad luck and you never know
You might be raking too.

Celtic Mary.

Oh Celtic Mary we'll miss you
A diamond you were through and through
We'll miss that smile and lovely face
And your memory we will sure embrace
You've lived your life, fulfilled your role
And you were such a lovely soul
Celtic woman to the core
And we think that you've been here before
Your journey isn't at an end
It's just a chapter, our good friend
And wherever you are now, I know
It was your time, you had to go
You'll aye be loved, and ne'er alone
We loved our Celtic Mary Sloan.

(*Author's Note* - My friend from Dunedin, Florida, Mary Sloan. I had swapped drinks here, and she hadn't noticed. Good times. Burns supper in Dunedin, 2015.)

Soulmate.

It's been such a long time since I saw your face
And a lifetime ago, since I felt your embrace
I miss you so much, after all of the years
And at night I still shed, a heart full of tears

You see, this is always how it was going to be,
You were the only, woman for me.
I sleep with your nightie, tucked under my head
And sometimes I picture you here in the bed.

I visit your resting place, and I kiss your stone
I want in beside you, I feel so alone
I tell you that I'll be joining you soon
Then we will be happy, just over the moon

I'll see your big smile, and you'll see mine as well
I've so much to talk off, so much to tell
So my darling dear wife, this poems for you
And it is simply a statement of a love so true

You were the best wife and mother,
Just ten out of ten
And I'll only be happy,
When I see you again,

For I love you so much,
Of that you should know

And I haven't been living,
Since you had to go

Again I tell you, this is how it would be
You were the only woman for me.

(*Author's Note* - This poem was written for an old
Gentleman who never got over losing his soulmate.)

The Scottish GI Joe (A Song).

Munros, Munros, he walked all the Munro's
He scaled the heights o' the man o' Storr
An everybody knows Munro's oh Munro's
He walked every Munro McGrandles o'
The 45 The Scottish GI Joe

There's a man that hails frae Fowkirk
Loved by one and all
He scaled the heights o' Scotia's hills
Frae Knoydart tae Glen Doll
Frae the Devils Point tae Etive Mhor
And The Cuillins oh sae braw
He seen the views that tak yer breath
The best ye ever saw

Chorus

He loves tae dae the bothys
He sings the ballads there
A wee bit dram doon by his side
His world not a care
A wee bit Kris Kristofferson
And the Eagles were his par
But when he does some Spear of Destiny
He's taken it too far

Chorus

Well McGrandles ta'en no weel
His legs dont work the same
He wonders how he'll manage
Withoot the Munro game

Dain Susan's heid in
In a lovely kinda way
And the lads frae the gallant 45
Would really like to say.......

That Paul, yer just a legend
And in the hills ye'll aye ways be
Coz we'll carry you there in oor hearts
The 45 degree

Wee Jimmy Fraz an Raymond Norrie
Allan George as well
The legends Frankie Reynolds
And John Mold wi tales tae tell

Munros, Munros, he walked all the Munros
He scaled the heights o' the man o' Storr
An everybody knows
Munros, oh Munros
He walked every Munro
McGrandles o' the 45
The Scottish GI Joe

(*Author's note* - This is a song I'd written for a friend, Paul McGrandles, who is suffering from MND at 50 years old.)

Ma Weans.

Awww, ma weans, they're just the best
I'm always nagging like a pest
Walk the dog please, dae ma dishes
Can't ye please just grant ma wishes?

Watch how you drive sir, you're no real
Two hands on the steering wheel
But I have tae nag, it's cause a care
An I couldnae love yees any mair

I'll watch ye grow, and watch ye learn
Even when it's no ma concern
And if ye think I'm nosey or bad
I'm no ony these, I'm just your dad

And one day in the future
When I'm no here tae bug yer brains
Just remember yer faither,
Ayeways loved his weans.

Carronshore.

It's just a wee mining village
No far fae Falkirk town
If ye ever get a wee bit time,
Take a wander down

It's got a bit o' history,
It's got a bit o' style
The best wee village in the land,
By a country mile

It's changed tho, it's not the same
Just life I guess, there is no blame
But for the purpose o' this rhyme
I'm gonnae take ye back in time

The Tarzan swing where we'd once play
Hours on end there we would stay
In all weathers, didnae care
We were content as we played there

The summer seats down by the shop
Where a' the men just had tae stop
Sometimes in all kinds o' states
Ha'in' a blether wi there mates
Wattie Begg, the shopkeeper there,
He wore a wee toupee for he had nae hair
He sold fish and chips on a Friday at night
Wi broon sauce an a pickle, what a delight

Gracie Doos shop, sellin' papers and fags
And ye didnae pay 5p back then for your bags

The Dock and the Vic, Blackmill and the Club
The Carronshore Bar, Nan Denovan's pub
The Liberal Hall where the weightlifters went
Givin' their all till their muscles were spent

Days and Innes, the bottom end shop
And the Gairdoch Inn where we had a wee bop
Ships used to come in and offload their stuff
Way back in time, when things were tough

As a wee village, ye couldnae want more;
The mining village of Carronshore.

Slàinte
Mhath

BIO.

My name is Douglas Marshall Smith, and I was born in the mining village of Carronshore, near Falkirk.
I love poetry and music, and have been writing poetry all my life. I turned 50 in 2018 and this is one of the things I promised myself I'd do.
The book is dedicated to my mum and dad, my kids, my brothers and friends who share my journey through this short life. I hope you enjoy the poems, songs and short story.

Thank you for reading

Dougie.

Notes.

Printed in Great Britain
by Amazon